AMERICAN MUSEUM
of NATURAL HISTORY

STERLING CHILDREN'S BOOKS
New York

An Imprint of Sterling Publishing Co., Inc.
1166 Avenue of the Americas
New York, NY 10036

ISBN 978-1-4549-3344-1

Distributed in Canada by Sterling Publishing Co., Inc.
c/o Canadian Manda Group, 664 Annette Street
Toronto, Ontario M6S 2C8, Canada
Distributed in the United Kingdom by GMC Distribution Services
Castle Place, 166 High Street, Lewes, East Sussex BN7 1XU, England
Distributed in Australia by NewSouth Books, University of New South Wales
Sydney, NSW 2052, Australia

For information about custom editions, special sales, and premium and corporate purchases, please contact Sterling Special Sales at 800-805-5489 or specialsales@sterlingpublishing.com.

Manufactured in China

Lot #:
2 4 6 8 10 9 7 5 3 1
04/19

sterlingpublishing.com

IMAGE CREDITS
Alamy: © Avalon/Photoshot License: 30, 31; © Andre Gilden: 18 (top), 23 (bottom); © Frans Lanting Studio: 28, 29; © Mark Levy: 25; © Luxy Images Limited: 13; © ozkan ozmen: 26 (top); © Ronald S. Phillips 20; © Paulette Sinclair: 2, 3; © Ann and Steve Toon 23 (top); **Getty:** © Arturo de Frias Photography: 8; **Minden:** © Michael and Christine Deni-Huot: 24; © Dickie Duckett: 14; © Richard Du Toit: 12; © Suzi Eszterhas: 9 (top), 11 (large); © Anup Shah: 12 (top), 15 (bottom), 22 (top); © Federico Veronesi: 9 (bottom); © ZSSD: 18 (bottom); **Shutterstock:** © MicheleB: 19; © Jordi C: 22 (bottom); © Danita Delmont: 7; © Keith Jenkinson: 11 (small); © Stepan Kapl: 27; © Theodore Mattas: front cover; 10; © Maggy Meyer: flap, 5; © Pablo77: 17; Paolino11: 26 (bottom); © Stuart G. Porter: back cover, 16; © PREJU SURESH: 21; © Sergey Uryadinikov:15 (top)

AMERICAN MUSEUM ᵒᶠ NATURAL HISTORY

Baby Lions Join the Pride

STERLING CHILDREN'S BOOKS
New York

Deep in the vast African grassland, two baby lions are born. A baby lion is called a cub. Most cubs are born in litters, or groups, of one to six.

The cubs are licked clean by their mother. Lion cubs are born with their eyes closed. They will stay closed for two to three weeks while the cubs remain under their mother's care.

The cubs are hungry! They drink their mother's milk.

When lion cubs are born, they weigh around four pounds. Adult female lions weigh around 280 pounds, and adult male lions can weigh around 400 pounds! Nutrients in their mother's milk will help the cubs grow into healthy young lions.

The male lion cub doesn't have a mane yet. He and his sister have grayish coats with spots that will disappear by the time they are about five months old.

Their eyes open and are a grayish-blue color. They stumble as they rise to walk, but two weeks later, they can run.

After two months, the cubs are ready to join the pride! A pride is a group of lions that live together. A pride can have anywhere between three and 40 members. Adults in the pride are mostly female, with usually just one or two adult males in the group.

The females, called lionesses, care for the cubs together. The cubs are nursed, or fed milk, from their mother as well as from other lionesses in the pride.

Lionesses hunt at night in groups of two or three. Since there are many to feed, lions typically hunt large prey like antelope, zebras, hippos, and wild hogs. They can take down prey in sizes that range from 400 to 1,200 pounds.

Their mother returns from a hunt. The lionesses have brought back an antelope. At three months old, the cubs can begin to eat meat! The adult lions eat first, and the cubs eat what is left over.

Male lions in the pride rarely hunt. Their role is to protect the cubs from hyenas and leopards, as well as from males outside of the pride that might try and take over.

A male lion's roar can be heard from five miles away. It warns intruders to keep away!

At six months old, the cubs have stopped nursing. They play and wrestle with each other under the hot African sun. Playing is important. It helps the cubs develop the skills they need to hunt when they are older.

The lioness cub tackles her brother to the ground! They tumble around in the straw-like grass.

Lion cubs make all sorts of noises. The playful cubs make cheerful "puffing" sounds. They team up and pounce at their friend, who answers with a startled "woof!"

At one year old, the cubs are as tall as their mother's shoulders. They are finally ready to help with the hunt! They join the group that goes out at night.

Lions are often not as fast as their prey, so they rely on teamwork and the element of surprise. That's why they hunt in the dark. They stalk their prey, following it closely, and pounce on it before it has time to escape.

At two years old, the cubs have become excellent hunters.

They are no longer considered cubs. They are young lions.

Young male lions usually leave the pride at two or three years old. For one to two years, they wander the grassland on their own or with other young males.

With no pride to protect him, the young male lion forms a coalition with other young males. A coalition is a group of young males that hunt together and protect one another while they search for a new pride.

At four years old, the young male lion is a full-grown adult with a big, shaggy mane. He has joined a new pride and has cubs of his own. He spends a lot of time lounging under the shade of trees.

As the sun is setting, the lion senses an intruder. He stands up and walks to the edge of the pride. He puffs up his chest and lets out a loud roar to protect his pride from danger.

Lionesses remain in the pride they were born into.

The young lioness now hunts with her mother and aunts. She helps the other lionesses care for their cubs.

When she is around four years old, she has a litter of her own. The pride will help her to protect and feed her growing cubs.